Holiday Songs From Arou...
CHRISTMAS TRIOS FOR ALL

Playable on ANY THREE INSTRUMENTS
or any number of instruments in ensemble

WILLIAM RYDEN

TABLE OF CONTENTS

INSTRUMENTATION

EL9566 - Piano/Conductor, Oboe
EL9567 - Flute, Piccolo
EL9568 - B♭ Clarinet, Bass Clarinet
EL9569 - Alto Saxophone (E♭ Saxes and E♭ Clarinets)
EL9570 - Tenor Saxophone
EL9571 - B♭ Trumpet, Baritone T.C.

EL9572 - Horn in F
EL9573 - Trombone, Baritone B.C., Bassoon, Tuba
EL9574 - Violin
EL9575 - Viola
EL9576 - Cello/Bass
EL9577 - Percussion

Editor: Thom Proctor
Cover: Dallas Soto

EL9566

ALPHABETICAL CONTENTS

WILLIAM RYDEN was born in New York City and is a life-long resident of Forest Hills, New York. He received his advanced musical training at The American Conservatory of Music in Chicago and at the Mannes College of Music in New York. The diversity of his composing ranges from solos to orchestra works, in both vocal and instrumental music. Since 1982 he has received 25 grants from the Meet-the-Composer Foundation. His numerous compositions and arrangements have been published by various prominent educational and performance music publishers.

WATT'S CRADLE SONG

PIANO/CONDUCTOR/OBOE

American folk tune

THE CHERRY TREE CAROL

England

THE MOON SHINES BRIGHT

England

THE FIRST NOWELL

France/England

REMEMBER, O THOU MAN

THOMAS RAVENSCRAFT 1611, England

WE THREE KINGS

JOHN H. HOPKINS 1857, America

AWAY IN A MANGER
(Second Tune)

Basque

WASSAIL SONG
(Here We Come A-Caroling)

England

WHEN CHRIST WAS BORN ON EARTH
(Song of the Bagpipers)

Italy

THE GOLDEN CAROL

England

PASTORES A BELÉN
(Shepherds in Bethlehem)

Puerto Rico

JOY TO THE WORLD

DR. ISAAC WATTS; attrib. G.F. HANDEL, England

BABE OF BETHLEHEM

THE SOUTHERN HARMONY

RISE UP, SHEPHERD, AND FOLLOW

Spiritual

HEAV'N BELL A RING

THE THREE KINGS

Flemish

Oboe

CHANUKAH SONG

Traditional Hebrew Song

DING DONG! MERRILY ON HIGH

France

Oboe

Allegro assai

* stagger breathing.

COVENTRY CAROL
(original 1591 version)

England

Oboe